A CATHEDRAL BUILDER

RANSKILL PRIMARY SCHOOL
CHERRY TREE WALK
RANSKILL
RETFORD
NOTTS. DN22 8LH

Macdonald

Contents

Introduction

This book tells the story of a boy called Etienne (Stephen in English) who was born in Rheims in northern France in about 1206. His father was a butcher, but Etienne preferred to spend his time reading and drawing. Not all boys of his time were taught to read; Etienne had been helped by the parish priest, since his father was not wealthy enough to employ a tutor for his children.

One day, a visitor to the butcher's house happened to catch sight of some of Etienne's drawings. He was very impressed by them, and suggested that Etienne might be able to make a career as an architect. Throughout France, great cathedrals were being built at this time. People from all walks of life gave money to pay for the vast stone buildings that towered above the wooden houses that surrounded them. They paid for famous architects and masons to design and build them, and for both the inside and outside of the cathedrals to be beautifully decorated with statues and carvings. People paid for these cathedrals to show their faith in God, and also because they wanted one of these fine buildings for their town.

The architects and masons who built these cathedrals belonged to a highly-trained, well-paid profession. They travelled round from site to site as work started on each new cathedral. Some, like Master Villard de Honnecourt, who appears in this story, were famous all over Europe. Many masons and architects made notes and sketches of buildings they had seen, or plans of buildings they hoped one day to construct, in notebooks. Some of these survive today. One of them, Villard de Honnecourt's notebook, has been used to help prepare this book.

In our story, Etienne's father has arranged for him to be taken on as an apprentice by the architect in charge of building Rheims cathedral. The story begins as Etienne is about to leave home to start his new life.

Some of the work and the tools of the medieval craftsmen are illustrated at the end of this book. In addition there are suggestions for places to visit and books to read.

A New Life

Etienne looked round the cosy dining hall. His whole family had gathered for a special dinner to say goodbye to him. He was surrounded by a cheerful, noisy crowd, chattering and laughing through his mother's excellent meal.

His father smacked his lips approvingly, as he finished a plateful of roast pork.

'Delicious!' he said. 'Sometimes I wonder why you want to leave home, Etienne. You couldn't be more comfortable! Everyone knows I run the best butcher's shop in town, and that your mother's the best cook for miles. But you want to leave us and fill your head with studying. You want to spend your life on cold, windy building sites, perched high above the ground on rickety scaffolding!' He smiled across the table at Etienne, who was frowning. 'Don't look so worried, we won't stop you going. It's a great ambition to be an architect. I'm very proud to have given money towards the cost of our new cathedral here at Rheims, and Master Jean, who's in charge of the building work, is very well respected – and well paid, too!' He laughed. 'So don't forget your poor old father when you're rich and famous like Master Jean!'

Etienne's mother interrupted him. 'Stop teasing the boy,' she said. 'I think he'll do very well. And now that his brothers are nearly grown up, we have all the help we need in the shop. Now, Etienne, are you sure you've packed all the books and papers that you want to take with you? It's nearly time to set off. We'll need to wrap up warmly in this snow.'

The opportunity for Etienne to leave home and start a new life had come about by chance. One day, when the bishop's secretary was visiting Etienne's father, he had noticed some of Etienne's drawings.

'Who did these?' he had asked. 'They're very good indeed! Would you mind if I showed them to one of our cathedral architects?'

Etienne's father was always quick to seize any opportunity that would help his family or his business. He had gone to see Master Jean himself, and had arranged for Etienne to be taken on as an apprentice. Today, he and his wife were going to take Etienne to meet Master Jean at the site of the cathedral.

The Masons' Lodge

Late that afternoon, at the building site, Etienne's parents said goodbye to him.

'I've signed the apprenticeship papers with Master Jean,' his father said. 'You know what that means. You have agreed to serve him for seven years, and to work hard and be obedient. Master Jean will provide food and lodging and clothes for you, and he and his workmen will teach you all they know. One day, you will be able to earn your living as a mason or, if you have the skill, perhaps you will even become an architect like Master Jean himself. Now, be good, work hard, and we shall all be proud of you!'

His parents hugged him goodbye and returned home without him.

Master Jean took Etienne over to the masons' lodge, and introduced him to a cheerful-looking man, who was busy measuring up a large block of stone.

'Robert is one of my senior workmen,' said Master Jean. 'He'll show you what to do.'

Etienne gazed in awe at the half-finished statues and beautifully-carved mouldings that lay all around. 'I'll never be able to carve as well as that,' he thought, in panic. 'Perhaps I shouldn't have come here?'

Robert's loud voice interrupted his worries.

'Come on, lad! Wake up! There's no time here for daydreaming! You can make yourself useful straight away. Take that broom over there and sweep up some of these stone chippings. The dust and grit get everywhere when we're carving.'

Etienne obeyed, but couldn't help feeling a bit disappointed. Had he left home just to do housework? But, in the days that followed, he found that he could learn a lot by watching the other men at work, and by asking questions. Robert was a good teacher. He showed Etienne how to hold a mallet and chisel, and let him practise on spare pieces of stone. It was as hard as Etienne had imagined it would be, but slowly he learned how to cut and shape the stone.

Robert made Etienne promise not to pass on his skills to anyone else. 'We stonemasons are very proud of our craft, and we don't want people making poor copies of our work,' he said. 'Only the best will do!'

Visitors

Carving stone was very painstaking work. Each block had to be slowly coaxed into shape, and then fitted into its precise place in the building. Often the masons used wooden frames to help them build a difficult shape like an arch. The frames were taken away once the final stone was hammered into position.

One day, as Etienne and Robert were working together on shaping some stone blocks, they heard the heavy rumble of cartwheels approaching and the clip-clop of horses' hooves on the stony road.

'Ah! that will be them!' said Robert, knowingly. 'I'd heard that Master Jean was expecting a visit. It's Master Villard d'Honnecourt, the architect. He's a great friend of his, but he's also a rival. He's working on the cathedral at Chartres, south of Paris. He and Master Jean always like to keep an eye on each other's work.'

'So that explains why Master Jean has been so cross recently,' said Etienne. 'He's been shouting at everyone; telling them to hurry up. He made a terrible fuss yesterday when old Hugh hadn't tidied up the masons' lodge as he'd been told to.'

'Yes, Master Jean likes his building sites to look as neat as possible. It's more professional, you see. And I

expect he's worried in case Master Villard will find fault with any of his designs. Villard's a great expert. He can tell whether an arch is sound, or whether a tower will fall down, just by looking at it. So can our master, of course,' he added hurriedly. Robert brushed the dust from his hands. 'Now, come along with me. We must help to welcome the visitors.'

Master Villard had arrived with a large group of followers. There were skilled workmen and apprentices, eager to learn and to observe, grooms to look after the horses, servants to fetch and carry, and last, but not least, a group of fierce-looking men-at-arms to protect the travellers from ambush by bandits on the wild, lonely roads.

Etienne was told to go and help Villard's apprentices to settle into their lodgings. One of them, Philippe, told him that his master often travelled round the country sketching down new building ideas.

In the Tracing Room

Master Jean was eager to discuss his new ideas for the cathedral with his visitors. The day after they had arrived, he took them across to the tracing room, where all the new designs for each section of the building were worked out. Each design was traced in a thin layer of wet plaster spread over the wide, level floor. Then carpenters made wooden templates from the tracings, and the masons used these as a guide to cut each stone very precisely.

The visitors listened while Master Jean pointed out various curves and lines on the tracing floor, and explained exactly how he wanted one particular arch to look.

'You're a clever man, Jean,' said Master Villard. 'Let me go and get my sketchbook to note down your ideas. I won't be long.'

While they were waiting for Master Villard to return, Master Jean started to discuss plans for a new doorway with the workman in charge of the tracing room. Etienne tried hard to follow what they were saying, but found that he couldn't understand. He picked up a bit of charcoal he found lying on the floor and started to doodle on a smooth patch of plastered wall. He began making patterns of curves and circles,

like those on the tracing floor, but it was much more fun to turn two of the circles into faces. Etienne was good at drawing, and the faces soon began to look remarkably like Master Jean and Master Villard. Etienne gave them silly expressions, and added a pair of horns to Master Jean's head.

He was so busy drawing that he didn't hear Robert calling him, until a handful of well-aimed stone chippings flew around his head.

'Come here when you're called, boy!' shouted Robert. 'It's getting dark and we must escort our visitors back to their lodgings. What were you doing over there, anyway? I couldn't see.'

Back at the visitors' lodgings, they sat round the fire, telling jokes and stories and drinking warm spiced ale. Etienne forgot all about his drawings . . . until the next day.

Pilgrims

Many visitors came to admire the half-built cathedral. Not long after Master Villard had arrived, a dusty group of pilgrims plodded wearily across the building site. They sang hymns and prayed as they walked, and seemed not to notice their blistered feet.

Etienne looked at them with great interest. 'Why have they come here?' he asked the bishop's secretary, who was passing by, with his arms full of papers.

'They have taken a vow,' he said, 'to go on a journey to certain holy places and to ask for God's blessing. They have promised to visit the shrines of twelve saints, including the shrine of our own blessed Saint Rémi here in Rheims. The holy relics of the saints will surely work their miracles for those who have travelled so far to see them.' The secretary made the sign of the cross, and threw a coin into a pilgrim's begging bowl.

Robert joined Etienne and whispered, 'He may give them alms, but it's the pilgrims who bring in the money to help build the cathedral.' He shrugged, 'But we need the money if we're to go on building. The local lords and townsfolk are very generous, of course, but building a cathedral costs a fortune!'

Just then, the chief stonecarver, Hubert, called sternly across for Etienne. He sounded very cross.

'You young fool!' he said. 'The master has just found your silly drawings on the tracing-room wall. He stormed out in a terrible rage and is threatening to send you back to your father.'

Robert shook his head at the news. 'You are one of our best apprentices. You could have a great future ahead of you. Why spoil it with stupid pranks? Go and find Master Jean and tell him right now that you are truly sorry!'

Etienne brushed away a tear as he walked over to Master Jean's room. 'Now I'll never be an architect or a mason,' he thought. 'I'll be sent home in disgrace.'

Master Jean was so cross that he lectured Etienne for almost an hour about respect and obedience.

'You will continue to work with Robert,' he growled, 'until I decide if you are to stay on as one of my apprentices or not. Now go! I am a busy man.'

The Journey Begins

One day, Master Jean strode into the masons' lodge.

'I want some volunteers to join me,' he said. 'Master Villard will be leaving us soon to return to Chartres. He must be back for the great feast of the Assumption on 15 August and he has asked me to join him for these celebrations. I plan to travel with him, first to Paris and then to Chartres. It is a wonderful opportunity to see two great cathedrals and to learn what we can from their builders. Robert will come with me and Hubert, but we need more masons and carpenters to travel with us!'

That was a week ago and today Etienne woke up feeling very excited. They were setting out on their journey this morning. He struggled into his boots and travelling cloak, and hurried down to the stables with Philippe. There the grooms were busy harnessing the slow, sleepy oxen to the great wagons.

Master Jean and Master Villard rode on fine horses, but the rest of the men clambered up onto the wagons and made themselves as comfortable as possible on some bales of straw.

After several days they passed a huge quarry. This was where the great slabs of limestone, used to build Rheims Cathedral, were cut out of the solid hillside. They stopped their journey to let Master Villard see the machinery that was used to move the heavy stone.

Etienne and Philippe rushed to peer over the edge of the quarry, ignoring Robert's warning to be careful. Far below, they could see men with picks and mallets, hacking out great lumps of stone and shaping them into rough blocks, ready to be hauled to the surface. A huge tower of scaffolding swayed in the gusty wind.

'Look, there's Robert!' cried Etienne, pointing to a tiny figure standing on the far side of the quarry. Robert was watching the men work the crane; they hauled on ropes that ran through a series of pulleys and down to the quarry floor. As they pulled, a huge block of stone inched its way up to the hilltop.

The boys heard footsteps behind them. Master Villard was setting himself down on a rock.

'Look!' said Philippe. 'My master has his famous sketchbook with him. What's he drawing now?'

Off to Paris

All too soon they were on their way again. The two boys chattered excitedly together long after the quarry had disappeared from view.

'If they let that great block of stone slip, it would fall and shatter into fragments,' said Philippe. 'And if they lost their footing, then the ropes would drag the men at the top of the cliff right over the edge. What a fall that would be!'

Just then, Etienne caught sight of Hubert's smiling face and grinned at him. It was the stonecarver that he had to thank for this trip. Hubert was pleased with Etienne's progress in stonecarving and felt that he would learn much from visiting other cathedrals. It was he who had talked Master Jean into taking the disgraced apprentice along, and he had promised to be the boy's teacher if Robert was too busy.

The journey seemed never-ending. The passengers' bones ached from the continual jolting of the wagon as the heavy wooden cartwheels lurched over the deep ruts in the road. But the boys soon forgot their bruises when they saw Paris lying ahead in the distance.

Hubert was as good as his word and proved to be a wonderful teacher. Once in Paris, he took Etienne and Philippe to see the magnificent cathedral. They arrived just in time to find a flurry of activity and shouting going on between some men at the foot of the cathedral and others perched high above on scaffolding. Suddenly all went quiet as the men above started to pull on some ropes. They watched, hardly daring to breathe, as a delicate statue was hoisted up into place.

Etienne was impressed with the work. 'I'll never be able to carve as well as that,' he said.

'Yes, you will,' said Philippe, encouragingly. 'Though I don't know why they've bothered. No one can see all that detail from the ground.'

Hubert could hardly believe his ears. 'Think what you're saying, child!' he said. 'We don't build cathedrals just to show how clever we are, or for men and women to admire. We build them for God and his angels. They can see everything!'

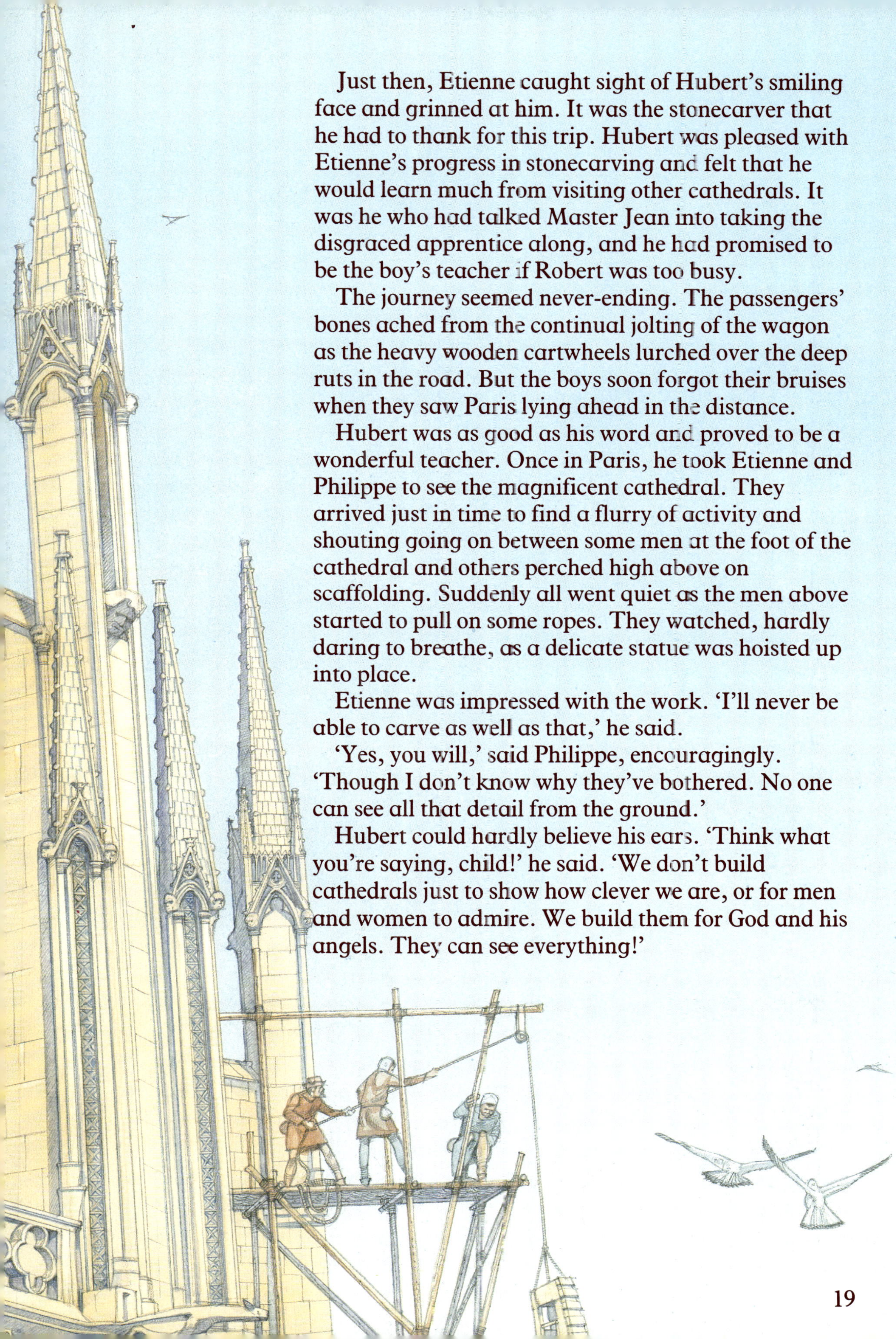

At the Fair

A great fair was held every year in Paris, and lasted for several weeks. Merchants came from all over Europe, bringing rare and precious goods to sell. Etienne gazed longingly at candied fruit and sweetmeats on the confectioners' stalls, but he knew he could never afford such luxuries. Robert marvelled at the gold and silver dishes displayed on the goldsmiths' stalls. 'Just look at that workmanship!' he exclaimed. He managed to strike a good bargain with a German locksmith who was selling some special iron locks that they wanted for the cathedral doors in Rheims. 'I know it's not much to look at,' said Robert, 'but this lock is a work of art, too, in its own way.'

Master Villard bought a new velvet robe lined with fur from one of the tailors. It looked very grand.

'He's going to demonstrate one of his new inventions here at the fair,' whispered Robert.

'What? Is Master Villard an inventor as well as an architect?' asked Etienne.

'It's all the same, really, if you think about it,' replied Robert. 'Architects have to invent all sorts of machines to help them construct the buildings they have designed. So why not invent other machines, too? Master Villard has brought what he calls his 'perpetual motion' machine with him to the fair.'

Etienne looked puzzled. 'His what?' he said.

'I'm not sure that I understand it completely,' said Robert, 'but I think the idea is to invent a machine that will go on working for ever and ever once it has got going, without needing any extra power. It looks rather like a wheel. You can see it over there.'

A crowd gathered to watch the experiment. Master Villard explained his invention and then, with a flourish, he gave his machine a gentle push to start the wheel turning. It spun round merrily a few times but gradually began to slow down. Finally, it stopped. The crowd burst out laughing.

Etienne saw Master Jean step forward and pat his friend reassuringly on the back. Etienne had seen little of his master on the trip so far; indeed, he had kept out of his way. Now he was reminded of the decision which still hung over his future.

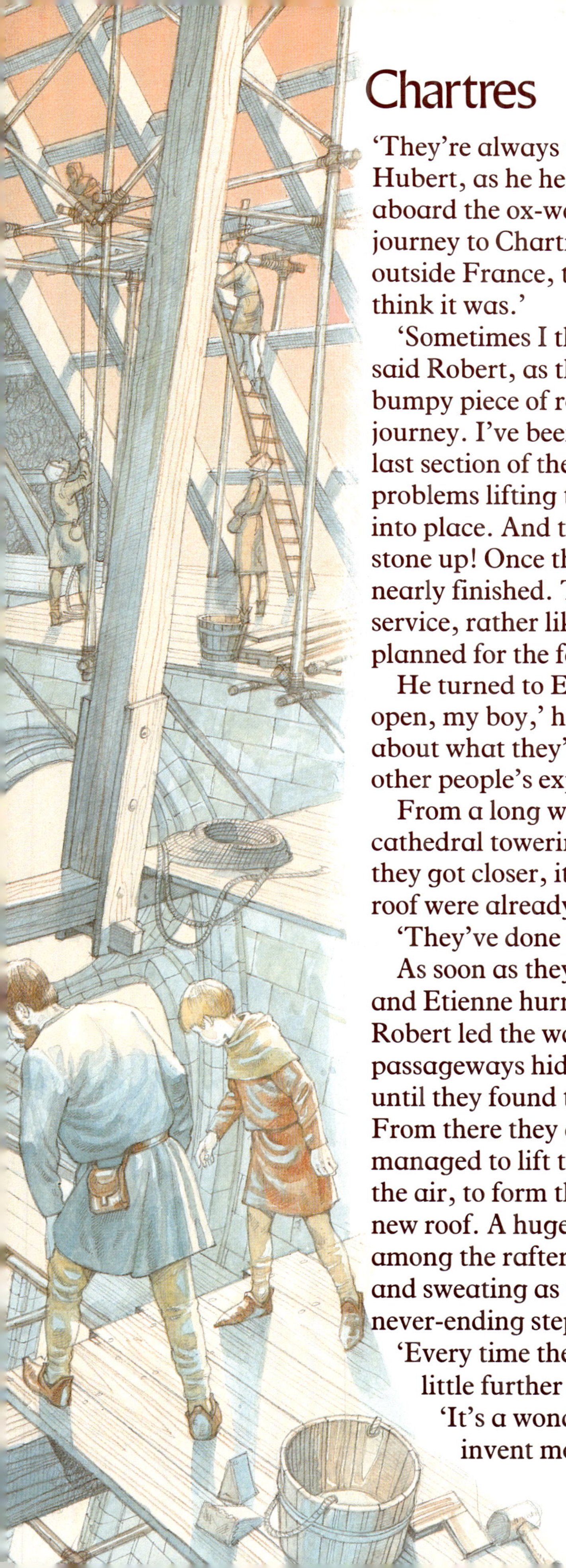

Chartres

'They're always travelling, these architects,' said Hubert, as he helped Robert and the boys clamber aboard the ox-wagon for the next stage of their journey to Chartres. 'Master Villard has even been outside France, to Hungary, to build a church, I think it was.'

'Sometimes I think all this travel is a bad thing,' said Robert, as the wagon lurched over a particularly bumpy piece of road. 'But Chartres is well worth the journey. I've been there before. They're building the last section of the roof now. I hear that they've had problems lifting the wooden framework for the arches into place. And that's before they try to heave the stone up! Once the roof is on, the cathedral will be nearly finished. Then there will be a great dedication service, rather like the procession and celebrations planned for the feast day.'

He turned to Etienne. 'Keep your eyes and ears open, my boy,' he said. 'Find out as much as you can about what they're doing. You can always learn from other people's experience.'

From a long way away, they could see the great cathedral towering above the houses of the town. As they got closer, it became clear that parts of the new roof were already in place.

'They've done it!' exclaimed Robert. 'But how?'

As soon as they reached the town centre, Robert and Etienne hurried over to the great cathedral. Robert led the way up a series of narrow steps and passageways hidden inside the walls of the building, until they found themselves on a narrow platform. From there they could see how the masons had managed to lift the heavy wooden frames high into the air, to form the arches which would support the new roof. A huge wooden treadmill had been built among the rafters. Etienne could see men straining and sweating as they took turns to 'walk' the never-ending steps inside the wheel.

'Every time they take a step, they lift the stone a little further off the ground,' explained Robert. 'It's a wonderful idea. If only someone could invent more machines to help us!'

Pictures in Glass

Etienne spent many days working among the masons and carpenters at Chartres before the feast day preparations began.

'I think I understand how it all works now,' said Robert, gazing for the hundredth time at the big treadmill.

He turned to Etienne. 'Have you noticed the stained glass that they are putting in the windows here?' he asked. 'It's wonderful! It glows like jewels when the sun shines, and there are pictures of angels and saints all singing and praying. It's almost like looking into heaven itself.

'The men who make the glass are clever craftsmen; I've never seen such beautiful colours before. Look at this rich, deep blue over here! Let's go over to the workshop and have a closer look while we're here.'

Patiently, the glaziers answered Etienne's long list of questions.

'First, we make a plan of how we want the finished window to look. Then we make sure that we have enough stock of all the different colours of glass that we'll need to make it. If not, then we have to make some more. There are secret recipes to mix each colour, and it's important to get the mixture and the temperature just right to make good glass. Once the glass has cooled and hardened, we cut it into the shapes we need to fit our plan. These are then fixed into place with thin strips of lead to build up each section of the window. We make the big windows up in sections like this in order to make them stronger.

'Most people can't read, so our windows tell the holy story in pictures. Sometimes they're called the poor man's Bible.

'There's not much work left for us to do on the cathedral now. Most of the windows are in place. We only have a few more windows to complete, and we've started work on them already. It looks as if our cathedral might be finished next year after all. If it is, then we'll have built it in under thirty years, and that's a miracle!'

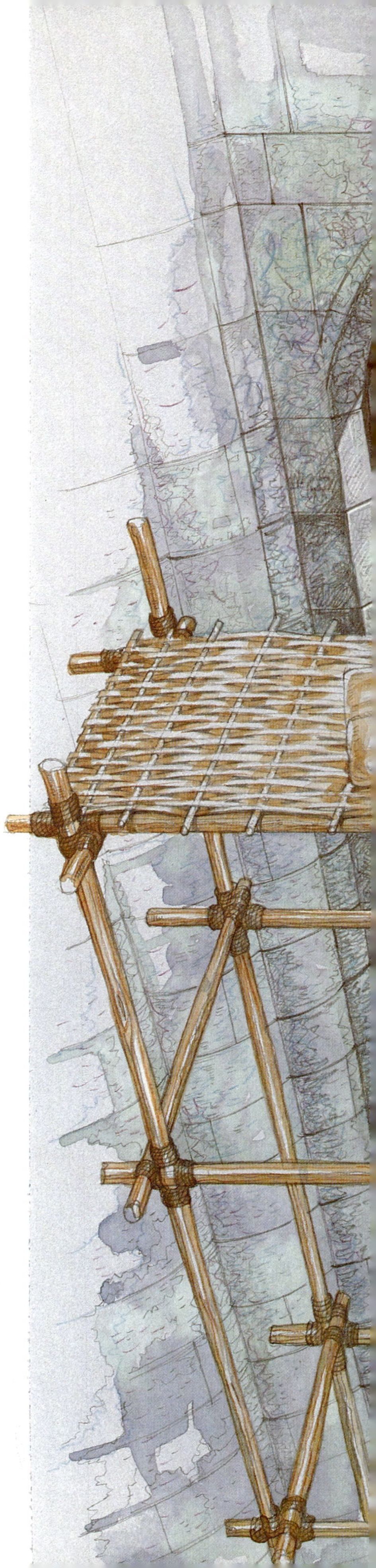

SANCTA ANNA

The Feast Day

All week there was an air of bustle and excitement as the townspeople made preparations for the great day of the Assumption. Many people travelled into town from outlying villages. Crowds jostled in the street. Priests practised carrying the unwieldy banners and statues that would form part of the solemn procession marking the beginning of the celebrations, when the holy relics of Chartres were carried through the town for all to see.

Etienne found it hard to join in the holiday mood. He felt miserable at the thought of their return to Rheims. Would Master Jean send him back to his parents in disgrace?

'Every day brings me closer to the end of all my

hopes,' he thought. 'I almost wish that Master Jean would make his decision now.'

But Master Jean was nowhere to be seen. When he did appear, briefly, he was always deep in discussion with Master Villard about the preparations.

At last the great day arrived. Crowds lined the streets by early morning, eager for a good view. Master Villard rushed around giving orders and checking every detail for the procession and the ceremony to follow.

Then, at last, Master Jean sent word to Etienne. He wished to see him.

'You know how cross I was,' said Master Jean gruffly. 'Well, I had decided that you should be sent home to your father on our return to Rheims.'

Etienne shuddered. His worst fears had come true.

'But,' continued Master Jean, 'Hubert tells me that you have worked hard and learned a great deal from this trip. He has persuaded me to change my mind. You may continue your apprenticeship, but keep your drawings in a sketchbook like Master Villard.

'Now, as a penance, I want you to come with me in the procession today to carry my heavy books and robes. It will be a long and tiring day, but you will have a splendid view.' He smiled. 'I'll be ready in one hour from now. Make sure that you are back here in plenty of time. Now, be off with you!'

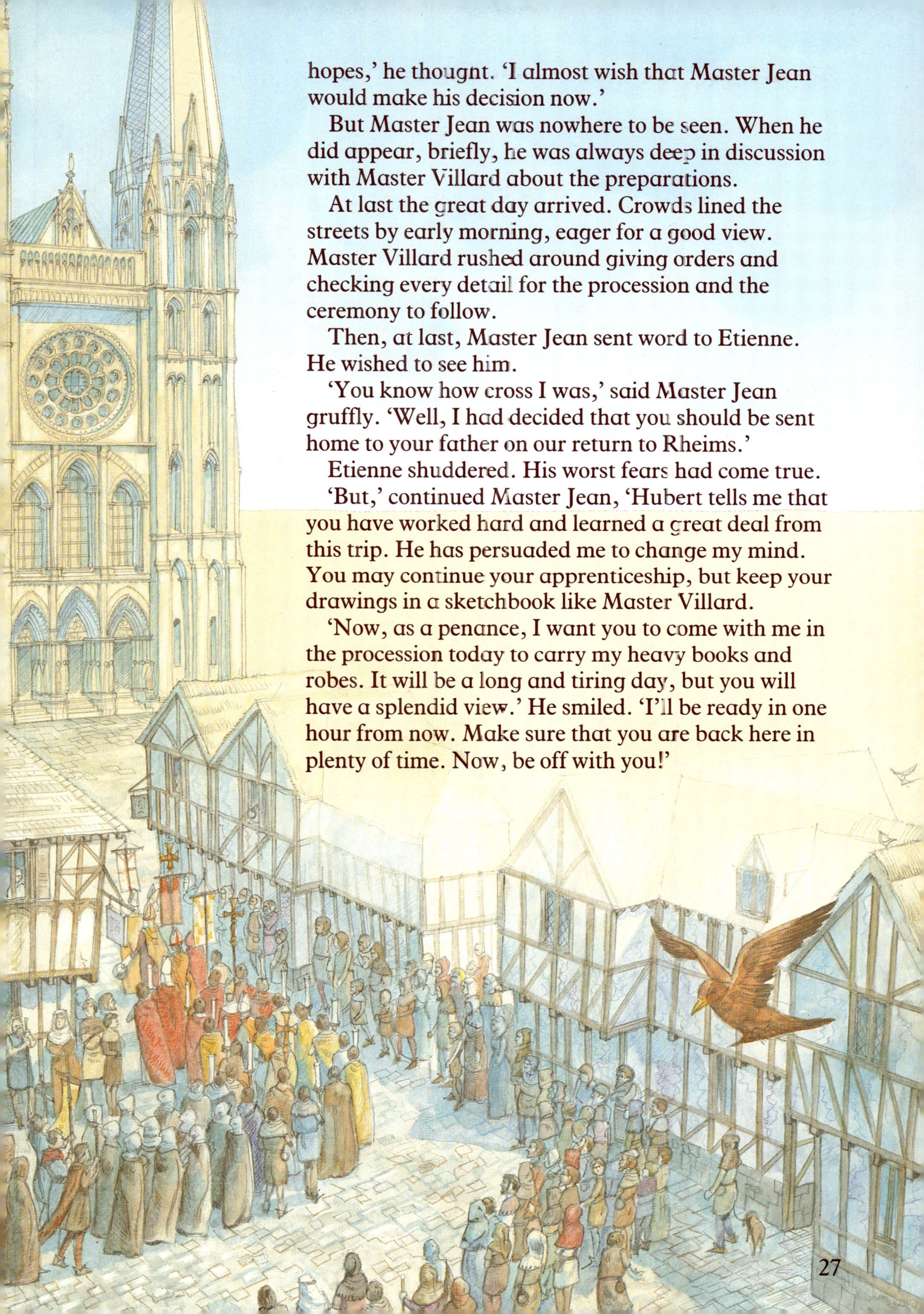

Picture Glossary

In many ways, cathedrals are just like other churches. They are used for religious services, for singing hymns and psalms, and for private prayer. Sometimes communities of monks live near by and worship there. Sometimes they contain the remains of a saint, and are a place for pilgrims to visit.

What makes a cathedral different from a church is that it also contains a bishop's throne, called a 'cathedra'. That is what gives it its name.

In the Middle Ages, many bishops decided that they wanted to build bigger and better cathedrals than the ones already existing. Money to build these new cathedrals came from local lords or townspeople, who gave money to the church because they felt it was a good thing to do, or to show how important their religious beliefs were to them. Sometimes they gave money to show how sorry they were for their past sins or in memory of someone dear to them. It was very expensive to build a new cathedral and took many years.

The buildings were designed and constructed by master masons and professional architects, who worked very closely together. We know about these people because some of them left notebooks with descriptions of buildings and detailed sketches.

Above: Rheims Cathedral
Building work started in 1211 and continued for over a century. Four different architects were involved in different stages of the construction. Originally, their portraits were carved inside the cathedral as a memorial to their work, but these portraits no longer exist.

Left: Blacksmith's workshop
Blacksmiths made all kinds of tools, nails, horseshoes and chains. They also sharpened and repaired tools damaged by the heavy work of stone quarrying and carving. In this picture, the smith is working at his furnace. The other two men are beating a hot metal bar into shape.

Right: Building craftsmen
Carpenters and masons worked side by side to build a wall. These men are using many of the tools shown in the drawings below, including a hoist, a plumb-line, an axe and an auger.

Left: Stonecarving
These beautiful statues from Chartres Cathedral are fine examples of master masons' skills. The stone has been carved to show the figures' flowing robes, long hair and beards in a very lifelike way.

Below: This special sign is a mason's mark. Each mason cut his sign into the stone to show that it was his work.

Right: A mason's tools
1 Dividers and set-square.
2 Stone-cutter's axe.
3 Tools for cutting and rough-hewing stone.
4 Plane.
5 Mallet.
6 Stone saw.
7 Star-chisel.

Right: A carpenter's tools
8 Sledgehammer and wedges.
9 Adze, to trim planks.
10 Spoke-shave, used to smooth planks.
11 Auger, used to make holes.
12 Bow-saw: the ropes keep the saw-edge taut.
13 Brace and bit, for boring small holes.

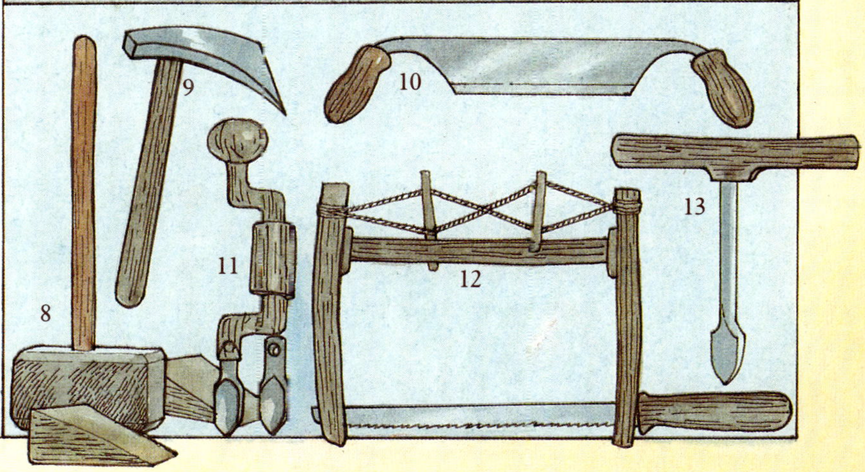

Finding Out More

Books to Read

The following books contain information about the Middle Ages and the building of cathedrals:

G. Caselli **The Roman Empire and the Dark Ages** (Macdonald 1981)
F. Macdonald **Everyday Life in the Middle Ages** (Macdonald 1984)
R. Unwin **Medieval Britain** (Hutchinson 1979)
P. Watson **Building the Medieval Cathedrals** (Cambridge University Press 1976)

You may need an adult to help you read the following books, but they contain a great deal of useful information:

J. Gimpel **The Cathedral Builders** (Michael Russell 1983)
J. Harvey **Medieval Craftmen** (Batsford 1975)
J. James **Chartres: The Masons Who Built a Legend** (Routledge and Kegan Paul 1982)

Places to Visit

The cathedrals mentioned in this book are all in northern France, but many cities in other countries in Europe have magnificent medieval cathedrals. Among the most famous in Britain are the cathedrals of York, Durham, Ely, Salisbury, Norwich, Canterbury, Gloucester and Exeter, also Westminster Abbey in London. Many beautiful parish churches also date from the Middle Ages. Masons would have been employed to help build them, too.

Many churches and cathedrals have stained glass windows surviving from the medieval period and there is a permanent exhibition of stained glass at Ely Cathedral, called 'The Stained Glass Museum'.